# TURNING MY PIECES INTO PEACE

Healing, Hope and Love for the Journey

JayMedia Publishing

Laurel, MD 20708

ISBN 978-0-9849290-6-1

# FORWARD

As much as I love experiencing the excitement of a good broadway play or seeing a well thought out dramatic plot unfold in a movie, I rarely live in a space of personal high drama or theatrics. It all changed however, when I stumbled upon the truth of my biological father and siblings while recreationally delving into my lineage. Make no mistake, the journey I will share does not resemble a fairy tale. This will be a transparent, real life journey through a traumatic discovery. As dramatic as that discovery was, it opened the door to a journey of hope, healing, love, forgiveness, encouragement and direction in a meaningful way. If you read my story and feel a connection, one thing is clear. You are not alone!

> Isaiah 43:19- Listen carefully, I am about to do a new thing,
> Now it will spring forth. AMP

# CONTENTS

Chapter 1

# SHOCK AND EXTRAORDINARY CIRCUMSTANCES
When a blessing doesn't really look like one

Two words describe what I have experienced. Life Altering! I felt the raw emotions of betrayal, and disappointment. I was heartbroken, and devastated by the revelation. For fifty-five years, five months and 27 days, I was secure in my own earthly family identity. I knew who I was because I knew who my parents were. I knew who my siblings, aunts, uncles, cousins, nieces and nephews were. At least, I thought I did. However, in that next moment, I had been unceremoniously uprooted like a tree and transplanted into another garden. My identity was shattered into tiny little pieces. It was unexpected, confusing, and heartbreaking beyond words. It was traumatic, plain and simple. I felt a sudden loss of a part of me. I was experiencing an identity crisis. I pinched myself to see if I was awake or merely experiencing a dream turned nightmare. These were just some of the emotions and thoughts that proliferated my mind, body, soul and spirit when I stumbled upon the truth. My dad was not my dad! My biological father was someone else. Who was I? I was in survival mode. Fight or flight. Those were my two choices at that very moment and in the coming days that followed. I chose to fight. Trees, no matter if they're large or small, will suffer some damage when uprooted from one garden and transplanted to another. But, prayerfully, with the proper care, they will survive.

In December of 2017, I gifted myself a DNA test for Christmas. I wanted to delve deeper into my ancestry. I wanted to know more about my roots. If Alex Haley could find his path back to Africa, I could surely find mine. February 27, 2018, 10AM, was an exciting moment. I had just received my Ancestry DNA test results back and I was ready to discover the regions of Africa my ancestors lived before the forced migration. The email from Ancestry DNA said, "You're about to discover your ethnicity estimate, get a unique look at your family's journey through generations, and maybe even connect with long-lost relatives. We're so excited for you!" I clicked open the first section. Wow! Benin/Togo, Cameroon, Ireland/Scotland, Mali and more. Now let's see if any of my relatives have taken this DNA test. I scanned quickly for known names. The only person I recognized was a second cousin whom I have known since she was a baby. I emailed her the great news that she and I were definitely related. When I scanned back to the top of the page, I read the following, "WP is your father!" What is this? It must be a mistake. My dad passed away a few years ago. And I was certain he never took a DNA test. I immediately exited out of the website and signed in again. I thought if I did, the website would correct itself. But, as I refreshed the page over and over again, I found myself staring at the same information. Parent/child relationship exists (confidence extremely high) match. I clicked on several different sections of information regarding the DNA test itself. I was attempting to make sense of it all. After several minutes of bewilderment, I snapped out of it long enough to look at the next few matches. The very next match was (SRob). He was listed as a close family to first cousin (confidence extremely high) match. I decided to send him an email. Within ten minutes, he returned my request. I could not even imagine what he must have been thinking. I could barely remember what I was thinking. We exchanged a few more emails:

Me: Good morning SRob, I just got my DNA results back. It says we are related. Do we know each other?

SRob: Good morning. I bet you have as many questions as I do right now. We don't know each other. I don't see anyone that I recognize on your tree. I don't want to play coy either because it appears we are very closely related.

Me: I agree. Emails back and forth just won't do. As you can imagine, I'm at a loss for words at the moment.

SRob: I would imagine you are at a loss for words. You read everything correctly as I did. (SRob attached his telephone number at the end of the email).

Me: Thank you for sharing your number. I will call you at 11AM.

SRob: Looking forward to hearing from you.

Oh my God! What was I thinking? It was 10:10 AM. I should have told him I would call him tomorrow instead of today! At least that would have given me some time to process the information I was reading on the Ancestry website. I began to pace the floor as I watched the minute hand tick by on the clock with what seemed like hours instead of minutes. The house was eerily quiet as I was home alone with these incredible thoughts and no one with whom to share them. Finally, at 10:58 AM, I sat down on the couch by the phone, anxiously waiting to make the call at exactly 11AM. My heart was racing as I tried to pull it together, so I could pick up the phone, dial his number and speak to this stranger on the other end of the line. When I dialed his number he answered immediately. We exchanged greetings after which I asked him his name. The stranger said his name was Shawn and he told me WP's name was Walter. I didn't recognize either. I then told him my mother's name and said he probably didn't recognize her name either. His response sent another jolt through my body. "On the contrary," he said. He had heard my mom's name spoken by Walter, a few years ago. The mystery was starting to unravel. My body was absorbing the shock of every word this stranger spoke. He told me that Walter had told him and his other siblings that they might have another sister out in the world, but he was not 100% certain of the paternity. "How are you related to Walter?" I asked. "He is my father." he replied. "So, you're my brother?" I asked. "It would appear so." he said. Shawn was not a first cousin. He was my brother. "Oh my God!" No other words came forth, just heightened anxiety and jumbled thoughts swirling around in my mind. My head was spinning. I was in a state of shock. I closed my eyes and covered my face with my free hand. Perhaps someone would shake or pinch me and wake me up from this unimaginable dream I found myself in. But it was not going to happen. I was living it, moment by moment. All the while, the strangers voice was calm, reassuring, loving, thoughtful, and caring. He told me to take all the time I needed to process this news. But I didn't need time, I needed answers!  We agreed to meet that week for breakfast so we could begin to sort out this crazy revelation. I have a biological father who is still alive? At this juncture, I'm still not completely convinced that this DNA information is 100% reliable. One might say I was in denial. After all, I did see one of my second cousins, who had also taken the DNA test, on my DNA tree. So many feelings and emotions were running through my mind. But the biggest question of all, at that moment, was why parents would conceal something as important as the existence of a child's biological parent(s). I had stumbled upon a new truth and I had to discover for myself the who, what, when, and why of it all. I was about to have my faith tested in the most peculiar way. The next few moments I looked in the mirror and saw a person I didn't fully know. I began pouring over pictures of my sisters and my parents, looking for the truth.

A few hours later, my husband Lee arrived home and I was able to share the news with him. He was quite calm as he listened to the story of my ancestry discovery. He was quietly but immediately concerned about my well being after this shocking news. He knew this could potentially be a monumental shift in both our lives and our son's life as well. I thank God everyday for my phenomenal husband. Who else could make me laugh in the middle of this storm, but Lee.

Psalm 34:18 The Lord is close to the brokenhearted and saves those who are crushed in spirit. (NIV)

James 1:2-4 Consider it pure joy, my brothers and sisters, whenever you face trials of many kinds, because you know that the testing of your faith produces perseverance. (NIV)

Chapter 2

## MEETING MY BROTHER

February 28, 2018, I was one day away from meeting my brother. We had exchanged pictures via text. In the days leading up to our meeting, I would look at his picture throughout the day and it would give me a moment of peace that I cannot explain. Perhaps it was because he was the only connection I had to an unknown part of my life. I would pray with intention that our first meeting be filled with God's love, grace, mercy, understanding, clarity, and everything else God had prepared in advance.

> Philippians 4:7 And the peace of God, which
> transcends all understanding, will guard your hearts
> and your minds, in Christ Jesus.

This was the day! March 1, 2018, I was on my way to meet my brother. I still can't believe I was saying those words, "My Brother." When I was a child, I wished for a brother so he could take my place in taking out the trash, walk me to the store, defend me when I was picked on. Well, you know, brother stuff. On my way to meet Shawn, I conjured up all sorts of thoughts in my mind and wondered what he would be like. Will I know right away that he is my brother? Would there be an instant connection? I wondered if we would really look like each other, or is he some crazy homicidal-suicidal maniac, or did AncestryDNA make a mistake? I was nervous beyond words. I prayed that God would take the wheel and get me to the meeting location in one piece. Whew! I finally made it! I arrived at the designated restaurant in Maryland, early enough to get a booth and strategically place myself in a position to see Shawn when he came through the front door. Minutes ticked by, but it felt like a lifetime waiting for him to arrive, and then it happened! He called me on my cell phone to let me know he was in the parking lot. As he entered the restaurant, our eyes met and we smiled at each other. It was a defining moment in both our lives. As he drew closer, the fact that he was my brother was confirmed. I could see his eyes were mine. There was something else that clearly spoke to me at that moment and said, "This is your brother." That inner voice could not have been anything else but the Holy Spirit speaking. With tears, and a heart filled with all sorts of emotions, we studied each others faces, hugged and sat down for what would become the longest breakfast meeting in the world. My heart was still racing. All I could do was stare in disbelief. It was an instant confirmation that we were related by DNA. Shawn pulled out his phone and showed me a picture of my paternal grandmother, who passed away in 2003. Wow! That was definitely an ah-ha moment. The uncanny thing was that not only did I look like her, I had my hair styled the way grandmother wore hers in the picture. It was clear that my large eyes and long lashes came from my paternal grandmother. Now I know the answer to the question I had asked so many times as a child while growing up, "What side of the family did my eyes come from?" Shawn then showed me a picture of my biological father. Again, wow! Another confirmation. He had his mother's (my grandmother's) large eyes and eyelashes as well. Shawn began showing me pictures of my other siblings. Oh yes, there are a host of brothers and sisters. It was clear to me with each picture that I was related to another family. I was a part of another family tree. I now have four new brothers and two new sisters who are all my biological father's children. I am the oldest in this group. Before February 27, 2018, I was one of three siblings. After that date, I became one of eleven siblings. I know, crazy! Sadly, two of the eleven, (two brothers), whom I will not get a chance to know, are deceased.

The food on the table was barely touched. We talked for hours about everything we could think of in those hours that might be important to know up-front. But everything was important. Everything was vital to the story of our brand new reality. Together we were creating a brand new beginning, and a brand new journey for us, our siblings, our parents, everyone. We both tried to absorb it all, in those moments, not missing a word spoken, or a curious, "I can't believe this is really happening," glance. The breakfast meeting left me mentally and physically exhausted. I experienced a wide range of emotions too complex to analyze. I didn't want our meeting to end. But it was enough information for the moment. One thing was certain. This would be one of many conversations my brother and I would have as we steered through this uncharted territory.

I experienced a rollercoaster of raw emotions. So many years missed. So much time unrecovered. I was excited and sad all at once. I felt happiness and anguish at the same time. I was excited and happy to finally meet this mystery person from the DNA website, who turned out to be my younger brother. I was relieved to finally find some answers. But, I was also disappointed and hurt that my mom hadn't equipped me with the truth at some point in my life.

I was in awe of how God had blessed me with an amazing little brother, who towered over me in height and who I loved instantly. I could only pray that my biological father, and my other siblings on this new family tree, whose roots run deep, would be as receptive to meeting me as Shawn had been.

God has an appointed time for everything. Although Shawn had been on the Ancestry website since the year 2000, it took eighteen years for me to create an account and discover his existence. Shawn said he always thought that if I was out in the world, I would try to find my lost family on the DNA website. The thought never occurred to him that I had no knowledge of a biological father and other siblings to search out. *I didn't know that I didn't know I was my parents' child.* There are lots of people in the bible who had to wait years to walk into their destiny. For example, Moses waited 40 years before he had his burning bush experience; Abraham and Sarah were in their old age before God blessed them with their son, Isaac; Joseph waited 17 years before he became the second most powerful man in Egypt next to Pharaoh; and King David waited 20 years to wear the crown; just to name a few. Although I waited 55 years to discover my biological father and other siblings, God knew when I was ready to receive this information. God chose that specific day in February to bless me in such a magnificent way and I will always and forever be extremely thankful and grateful. He prepared my heart ahead of time to receive and I just don't have the time nor the energy to waste being angry, precious time I could spend getting to know my new family.

The next steps of this remarkable journey would be to talk to my mother and to meet my biological father. I asked the Lord to speak to me about when and how to talk to them.

2 Samuel 22:31a As for God, his way is perfect. NIV

*Romans 8:28 And we know that in all things God works
for the good of those who love Him, who have been called
according to His purpose. NIV*

On March 2, 2018, Shawn telephoned me to let me know he had spoken to our father and that he indeed wanted to meet me within the next couple of weeks. I wanted BF to know that I wasn't angry and I prayed that he will receive me as the person I have grown to be. Shawn  helped to set up our first meeting.

The next few days I began to wonder how my mom and biological father met. I wondered how my two childhood sisters would react after hearing this breaking news and how my mom and biological father as well as new siblings would respond to this news. As much as this had been life changing for me, they would have to navigate this extraordinary occurrence as well.

I also contemplated how my son would react to finding out he has a grandfather, although I think I know the answer to that question.

Chapter 3

## MY TALK WITH MOM

On Sunday, March 4, I arrived at my mother's house to have "the talk." At this point, she had no idea that I had taken a DNA test or that I knew her secret. I walked in with groceries from the market for her, as well as lunch. After we ate, I told her I had something important I needed to talk to her about. She seemed intrigued. I calmly and gently told her I had taken the DNA test through Ancestry hoping to find my African roots. Although my results revealed percentages of a variety of ethnicities, the results also revealed that a man named Walter was my biological father. She had a look on her face of shock and dismay. Her one word response was, "What?" After several seconds passed, she began to acknowledge my discovery and explain to me what, when, why and how this all came to be. After her explanation, I told mom that I forgave her. But I was disappointed that she could not have found a time in my adult life to tell me. I didn't ask mom any more questions because I wanted to give her an opportunity to digest the shock of me knowing the truth.

As hurt and disappointed as I was by this ordeal, I knew it was important for me to forgive my mom. I needed to forgive her not for her sake, but for my own peace of mind. Unforgiveness breeds nothing positive in one's life. Who am I to judge anyone? Jesus graciously has mercy on me everyday of my life. And His word is clear.

> Luke 6:37 says, "Do no judge, and you will not be judged.
> Do not condemn, and you will not be condemned.
> Forgive (pardon), and you will be forgiven.

Just because I forgave my mom did not mean the hurt that I felt would go away automatically. My recovery would take time; my healing would come through much prayer laced with God's love. The fact is I'm a human being with real feelings and emotions and not a robot manipulated by a switch, toggle or button. I don't know how long this healing process will take, but, I am hopeful in Christ, that the hurt will, in time, dissipate. My prayer is that God will continue to guard my mind, heart, soul and emotions and that He will continue to cover me on every side of this journey.

> *Isaiah 43:2-3 When you walk through the waters, I will be with you; and when you pass through the rivers, they will not sweep over you. When you walk through the fire, you will not be burned; the flames will not set you ablaze. For I am the Lord your God, the Holy One of Israel, your Savior. (NIV)*

If you are a parent who is connecting with my story on a personal level, I pray that you garner the courage to speak the truth to your child concerning something as important as the circumstances of his or her birth. In an age of scientific advancement and modern technology, the truth will eventually surface and your child will more than likely experience the hurt and pain of your secret. It will not only affect your child's life, but yours as well, and perhaps many other people connected directly or indirectly to that revelation. Do everything, as much as it depends on you, to prevent your child from being blindsided by this life altering event. Choose to walk them through it rather than allowing them to experience this moment on their own.

> *1 Chronicles 22:13b Be strong and courageous. Do not be afraid or discouraged. (NIV)*

Chapter 4

## TAKING CARE

The morning after my talk with mom, I was feeling out of sorts. I decided to take a walk and talk to my girlfriend and confidant, Alicia. My idea of normal had been shaken to its very core. Alicia explained to me that I was feeling the aftershocks of experiencing a significant emotional incident. In other words, I had experienced a traumatic event. She was right. I did feel like I had been put through what felt like an enormously powerful earthquake followed by waves of emotional tremors deep inside my core. I felt mentally and physically broken. It had only been a few days since my discovery and my mind and body, currently in conflict with each other, were trying to reconnect. It felt like I was in a sci-fi movie and having an out of body experience. My mother texted me and said she wanted me to be at peace. My brother Shawn telephoned me and said he wanted me to be at peace. Therefore, peace was the word for the journey that day. My God is the God of peace, rest and contentment. I'm praying that He will keep me safe, well, and whole.

*Philippians 4:7 ...and the peace of God, which
transcends all understanding, will guard your hearts
and your minds in Christ Jesus. (NIV)*

*Isaiah 26:3 You will keep in perfect peace whose mind is
stayed on You, because he trusts in You. (NKJV)*

On some level I was very likely experiencing a form of PTSD (post-traumatic stress disorder). According to an article in the New York Post, written by Eric Spitznagel, this discovery has spawned its own unique syndrome called PTDD (post-traumatic DNA-test-results disorder). I decided to seek counseling.

I needed to understand the process to go through so I could begin to feel my "normal" self again. Whatever that was. At my first appointment, the counselor was just as shocked as I had been when I told her of my biological parent discovery. Hilarious! I'm not sure if professional counselors are used to patients who are dealing with news of this nature. However, with the advent of DNA testing, counselors need to get ready and be ready to work with people experiencing this type of trauma. The counselor I visited advised me to journal and consider writing a book. Funny! I was already journaling as a form of therapy. I figured that journaling would help me get it all out of my system if I put my thoughts and feelings on paper. I was also told by three other people to write a book, so, here we are! I realized that it would be a process that could lead to a new normal for me. I also realized that I would be making an impact on the world by helping others who are like me. They could boldly tell their stories so they could heal and live a blessed life, no matter what the circumstances may be.

I knew it was crucial for me to take care of my mind, body, soul, and spirit so I could remain healthy. I also knew it was important for me to seek professional guidance in this matter, in case it became too overwhelming for me to handle on my own. I was not concerned about what others might think of my seeking counseling and I was not at all embarrassed about my decision to do so. I was doing it for my own peace of mind, health and welfare. I experienced symptoms that validated my decision including loss of appetite lasting several weeks and an anxiety attack which sent me to my physician. Let's be real! My identity had been shattered and my mind, body, soul and spirit were trying to process some unbelievable information. There was a whole other half of me that I don't know. I admit it; I felt lost. As I looked up and cried out to my heavenly Father, He drew me closer to Him than I could have ever imagined. He knew exactly what I needed.

> Psalm 121:1-2 says; I lift up my eyes to the mountains--
> where does my help come from? My help comes from
> the Lord, the Maker of heaven and earth (NIV)

God surrounded me with His love, comfort, protection, healing, and so much more throughout this entire journey. I am in love with the extremely close relationship I have with my heavenly Father right now. God promised, in

His word, to never leave me or forsake me. I'm a living witness that He has been true to His word my entire life. When I've felt my weakest, His grace is sufficient. God has also placed special people in my life to help me navigate this process.

*Proverbs 27:17 As iron sharpens iron, so one person sharpens another (NIV).*

I know that God has equipped me, in advance, for this new journey as He leads me along the way.

*Psalm 119:105 says, Your word is a lamp for my feet, a light on my path (NIV).*

I began exercising more and resting when I felt too tired to deal with any additional information. Prayer, reading God's word, meditation, eating healthy, physical exercise, laughing, singing, dancing, or enjoying a favorite fun activity also helped alleviate stress and anxiety. I found the positive activities that I knew would help reduce my stress level and put me back on track. These activities really helped me physically, mentally and spiritually. I did any positive activity God showed me to strengthen my positive outlook.

*Philippians 4:8 Finally, brothers and sisters, whatever is true, whatever is right, whatever is pure, whatever is lovely, whatever is admirable, if anything is excellent or praiseworthy think about such things. (NIV)*

I find that it is difficult at times to not think about all the years that I have lost with my siblings and biological father. I wonder how it could have been to be in their lives and they in mine. They are all younger than me. I imagine I could have been looking out for them, taking the younger siblings on outings like the zoo, to the amusement park, and just doing what big sisters would do with their younger siblings (Laughter). They have history, routines, and traditions that I know nothing about. I pray that God will show me how I fit in with my new family. I know that there is nothing I can do about those missed years. I can only make the decision to look towards the future with a thankful heart and build relationships with each of them. I am ever so hopeful that the best is yet to come. Romans 5:3-5 says suffering produces perseverance, which produces character, which produces hope.

Chapter 5

## MEETING MY BIOLOGICAL FATHER (BF)

Two weeks had passed since my life changed forever and the meeting had finally been set. Shawn had arranged for BF and me to meet, for the very first time, on March 15, 2018. There was no turning back now! Whatever happened, I knew that all things work together for my good because I love the Lord and I know I have been called according to His purpose, and I know God loves me. I choose to put my trust in God and His word. He is my loving Father and He knows what's best for me.

It was the evening of March 14, 2018. In less than 24 hours, I would be meeting my biological father for the first time and I wasn't sure how I felt about it. Perhaps I was a bit apprehensive since I didn't know what to expect or how I would be received. I was also thinking that I didn't want to be disappointed. I began wondering if I would like him right away or would my biological father like me. Would he love me? There was an entire half of me that I knew absolutely nothing about, but I needed to complete my life story. One thing I did know with certainty - God had orchestrated it all. I thanked Him for allowing me the opportunity to meet my biological father. I was also thankful that my brother Shawn would be at the meeting as well.

This must be awfully strange and somewhat difficult for Shawn, too. I realized that this discovery had affected him as well. I asked Shawn what his reaction to my discovery was like for him. He told me that after his initial surprise, he was more concerned about me and BF than about himself. Dealing with the science of the DNA process, it was a fact that I was his sister. He said it was hurtful to think that I had been here for all those years without having an opportunity to have a relationship with all my siblings, especially the two deceased brothers. The day we finally met, Shawn said he was very nervous and didn't know what to expect, but that thus far it had been a totally pleasant experience. Other than that, he said, "I've got another sibling to keep up with." Shawn would be one of the many siblings who would have to process this life change in the weeks to come.

March 15, 2018, turned out to be quite an extraordinary day. After arriving at the breakfast meeting, Shawn and I walked over to our father's vehicle. I was nervous, apprehensive, and excited all at once. Once BF stepped out of his vehicle, I looked directly into his eyes and said, "Surprise!" It was my attempt to break the ice right away. He responded with laughter. We went inside the restaurant and sat down in a booth on opposite sides, facing each other. We were two strangers, but not really strangers at all. He possessed the other half of my DNA. He began to speak and asked me the questions that must have weighed heavily on his mind. He asked, "How was your childhood?" I said, "It was good." "Were you treated well?" I said, "Yes." "Did you have a good life?" I said, Yes, I did." I was thinking to myself that there was so much more behind his questions and my answers but it would take a lifetime to unfold our exchange. After all, he knew nothing about me nor I about him. He had a look of genuine concern on his face. He seemed relieved that I answered the questions to his satisfaction and that my answers were all positive. Once these initial questions were seriously asked and answered, the remaining time was filled with laughter as I discovered the source of my funny bone. Growing up, I loved to make people laugh, especially the family. My BF has an over-the-top sense of humor. I observed a kind, handsome and funny older individual whose eyes were my eyes. At the conclusion of breakfast, Shawn and I walked BF back to his car. He extended his hand to me, perhaps not knowing what else to do. I immediately dismissed his hand and gave him a hug to let him know, no matter what has occurred in the past, we are family.

I thanked God for allowing me to break bread with my biological father and brother that morning. I could not have done it without Him. Thank you Lord. Your love for me is beyond my comprehension and beyond what anyone can fathom. I looked forward to getting to know this man for myself. I looked forward to introducing my son to his grandfather, and my husband to his father-in-law.

I choose Isaiah 61:1-3 - "Beauty instead of ashes, the oil of joy instead of mourning, and a garment of praise instead of a spirit of despair." (NIV)

Chapter 6

## MY SON'S PIANO RECITAL

Saturday, March 17 had arrived and despite all that had transpired in the past three weeks, life still went on. On this day my son, DJ, had a piano recital. Several of his current aunts and cousins, including my mother, would be in attendance. DJ proved once again that practice makes you a better pianist as he did an outstanding job playing his original piece and a piece selected by his music teacher. Of course, I'm not biased at all. Once the recital concluded, we all travelled down the road to breakfast at the Nautilus Diner. The tension in the room between my mom and me was palpable. We were all seated at the same large knights-of-the-round table. My husband, my mom and I were the only three people at that table who knew the truth I had uncovered. I suddenly had an out of body experience. I saw myself at the table, holding a mic and saying, "I have an announcement to make! Mom, don't you have something you want to say?" This is an example of how the enemy plays with your mind. I knew in my spirit that I would never embarrass my mother or shock my sisters in that fashion. Instead, everyone enjoyed a delicious and drama-free breakfast and fellowship. The gathering concluded with a wonderful thank you speech by my son, the musician.

While I felt sad about the current state of affairs, I knew my loving Father in heaven would have so much more in store for me so I pressed forward to enjoy the time I now had with my biological father and my new family members, should they desire to be a part of my life.

> Psalm 143:8 Let the morning bring me word of your unfailing
> love, for I have put my trust in you. Show me the way I should
> go, for to you I entrust my life. (NIV)

Chapter 7

## SIBLING SUPPORT & THE BIG REVEAL

On the evening of March 19, I received an unusual text from my eldest sister, Linda. She wanted to know if I had any plans for the following day. That alerted me that mom finally told her and my younger sister, Joann, the news. The text stated that the two of them wanted to come over the next day and give me some "sisterly love." Growing up, Linda and Joann had always been especially close. I thought they would need each other more in the coming weeks as they dealt with the new realities of life as well. On March 20, Linda and Joann stopped by my house to check on my welfare and to tell me of their conversation with mom. The past Sunday afternoon, mom surprised them with the information that I had a different biological father. When Linda heard the news from mom, she said that she just sat there, listened and took it all in. Joann said when she heard the news, a migraine immediately ensued. Joann asked mom if the father she grew up knowing was indeed her father and the answer was yes. Linda said she understood why I was not told as a child, however, mom should have told me at some point in my adult life. They said they came over to make sure I was okay. I was doing as well as could be expected under the given circumstances. As the song goes, "One day at a time, sweet Jesus." While we were talking, Shawn telephoned to let me know that my BF communicated with his other children that they had another sister. Oh to be a fly on the wall at that moment. I was relieved that everyone now knew. Moving forward in Christ!

Chapter 8

## MY GREAT PLAN

The following day, I received a phone call from my new-found sister, Bobbie. She seemed quite pleasant on the phone. Shawn had shown me some pictures of her. There was a definite resemblance between Bobbie and me. The following evening, while on my way to tennis practice, I received a phone call from my new-found brother Loren. He said he was the quiet and mild-mannered sibling. His tone sounded like that of an older brother. We had a very pleasant conversation. I looked forward to meeting him as well.

Bad news! While playing tennis that evening, while stepping backwards for a lob I lost my footing and landed on the back of my left hand and fractured a bone in my wrist. I guess I just lost my focus while moving on the court. Hmmm, I wonder why? The doctor said I would have to wear a cast for six weeks. I'm a pretty active person so I knew this injury was going to be tough. I was going to have to figure out how to get in my exercise. This was not a time for me to be inactive. Ugh!

God placed in my heart the idea of having an official "Siblings Fellowship" at my home to bring together my "old" siblings and my "new" siblings. I wasn't sure if everyone would come but I was praying that they all would. It would be a great opportunity for my two sisters to meet my new brothers and sisters, and vice versa. I had the day pictured in my mind. It would play out similar to the big celebration scene in the movie, "Antwone Fisher." There would be lots of good food, fun, fellowship, and whatever else God had in mind for this special occasion. The date was set for Saturday, April 14, at 4pm.

On Saturday, March 24, 2018, Shawn arrived at my house to meet my husband, Lee, and my son, DJ, for the first time. Shawn had one of his sons with him as well. But there was another vehicle that followed him to my address. Shawn said he had a surprise for me, my new sister Bobbie appeared from the second vehicle. What a welcome surprise. Oh my gosh! Bobbie and I look so much alike. They came inside and we all sat down in the family room for a little fellowship. Bobbie has a sweet soul. She was quite shy as she sat next to her -- I mean, *our* brother. After all, it was our first face-to-face encounter. I can't get over how much she looks like me. What an eerie feeling. I just kept thinking that I could have gotten to know them long ago, instead of now sitting across from two strangers. But I know that was not God's plan for me. And God has perfect timing. So, I will continue choosing to lean on my perfect Father in heaven and not on my own understanding.

> Proverbs 3:5-6 Trust God from the bottom of your heart; don't
> try to figure out everything on your own. Listen for God's
> voice in everything you do, everywhere you go; he's the one
> who will keep you on track. Don't assume that you know it all.
> (MSG)

Chapter 9

## MOM'S ACTING WEIRD

We were all at a retirement function later that evening after Shawn and Bobbie left.

My mom was acting really weird. She avoided talking to me the entire night. I decided I would have to give her some time and space to process this new reality. I believed she needed some adjustment time just like me. I couldn't imagine the emotions she was experiencing knowing that she kept this information from her child for all these years. But, my prayer was that she would be able to talk to someone who could help her work through her own pain. Shawn told me that I needed to call my mom often and reassure her that I had forgiven her, that I had moved forward, and that she needed to do so as well.

Wouldn't it be lovely if life were that simple. It sounds good on paper, but, the truth is that  although I have forgiven her, I didn't feel the capacity in my heart, at that moment to completely move beyond my own pain. It wasn't that long ago that I discovered the truth. This is a marathon and not a sprint. This is a journey that I'm taking with the Holy Spirit as I recover. I know that God will help mom and me mend our relationship because that is my desire as I continue to put my trust in Him. I know that God will do it. I love my mom with the love of Christ. She raised me and my two sisters to be the women we have become, and I am grateful to have her in my life. I am certain that as I wait on the Lord, He will renew our relationship.

Isaiah 40:31 But those who wait on the Lord shall renew their
strength; They shall mount up with wings like eagles, they
shall run and not be weary, they shall walk and not faint.
(NKJV)

I needed a break! I would have loved to take a few days and run away by myself so I could get a little peace and perspective. But, I don't think I could've made it too far with that pink cast on my arm. I chuckled at this because I know God knew in advance that I would try. As I wrestled with these feelings, I knew that my God is perfect, He always knows what's best for me, and He has perfect timing. I know that I can lean on Him for rest and renewal. I can throw all of my burdens on Him and in return He will provide me with His perfect rest.

> Matthew 11:28-30 Are you tired? Worn out? Burned
> out on religion? Come to me. Get away with me and
> you'll recover your life. I'll show you how to take a real
> rest. Walk with me and work with me--watch how I
> do it. Learn the unforced rhythms of grace. I won't lay
> anything heavy or ill-fitting on you. Keep company with
> me and you'll learn to live freely and lightly. (MSG)

Therefore, I will continue to move forward on my journey, in constant fellowship with God, knowing that He will take all of these pieces and add much more laughter, love, joy, and peace as I get to know and experience this new chapter in my life with BF and my new siblings.

> Hebrews 12:2 Let us run with perseverance the race
> marked out for us, fixing our eyes on Jesus, the pioneer
> (author) and perfecter of faith. (NIV)

## Chapter 10

## TO GRANDPA'S HOUSE WE GO

On March 28, Lee, DJ and I drove to BF's house so that DJ could meet his grandfather for the very first time. DJ has often said to me that he wished he had a grandfather. He used to tell me that he missed my dad. I always found this to be odd since the dad who raised me passed away before DJ was born. Perhaps he could feel a missing piece in his life as well. I am so thankful and grateful that God, in His infinite wisdom, love, and grace, has filled a desire in my son's heart. What a wonderful blessing and what a wonderful Father in heaven. He knows what we need even when we don't know what we need.

When we arrived at BF's house, I looked up and down the street, imagining what it would have been like to grow up in this area, running and playing with my other siblings. The three of us walked through the gate, past the lovely little garden, and up the gray cemented steps. I opened the white screen door and we proceeded onto the wood landing. The front of the house had a screened in porch with a swing, hanging plants, and a ceiling fan. It looked like one of those porches where you could just spend a lazy day hanging out, sipping lemonade, swinging, laughing and people watching. I rang the doorbell and waited for BF to open the door. Once I crossed the threshold into the living room, it felt quite erie to be inside this home for the very first time. This was the childhood home of my other siblings, the home they grew up in, laughing, learning and loving. At first glance, I noticed all the childhood pictures of my siblings at various stages of their lives perched in various areas between the living room and dining room. The only picture I could see missing from the equation was my own.

DJ greeted his grandfather with a "hello grandpa," and they hit it off right away. To my surprise, my new sister, Adrienne and her daughter were there as well. Adrienne was very emotional and teary-eyed. We hugged as we greeted each other, then sat down in the dining room and talked for a while. Adrienne and I had a great first conversation. Staring at each other, I could see that we both had the same smile. She has such a big heart. She was definitely concerned about me and wanted to make sure I was doing okay. My response was, "As well as can be expected under these extraordinary circumstances." Moving ahead, I'm looking forward to developing our relationship.

It is April 5, and we were getting closer to the siblings fellowship at my home in Maryland. Whenever I talked to Shawn or Adrienne on the phone, I felt as though we were all trying to make up for lost time. I know I was, but I think they were as well. They texted or called to check up on me often. It was a blessing to know that they were genuinely concerned about my welfare. Even now, I think we are all in the, "what now?" phase. We are trying to figure out how I fit in and how they fit in this new family dynamic. I'm certain it will be quite a journey of discovery. I think the best thing we can all do right now is to just be ourselves and see where the Lord takes us. This is still all quite surreal to me at this point.

*Proverbs 3:5 Trust in the lord with all your heart and*
*lean not on your own understanding. (NIV)*

My journal entry for Tuesday, April 10, 2018, reads as follows; "Six weeks ago I found my brother on Ancestry and life has never been the same." After six weeks, it still felt like an episode of "The Twilight Zone," where I've entered another dimension. I'm working on not letting the feelings of disappointment and sadness over lost time with family get in the way of progress. I know I didn't find my family by accident. God chose that day in February, that place, that time, and that moment to reveal to me the other part of my DNA. It was a divine appointment. I can't wait to see how this all plays out next Saturday. I was bringing two families together for the first time. I prayed to God that He would overshadow my home and that everyone who crossed the threshold Saturday, would enter with love, mercy, and grace in their hearts.

1 Corinthians 2:9 Eye has not seen, nor ear heard, Nor have entered into the heart of man the things which God has prepared for those who love Him. (NKJV)

Chapter 11

## SIBLINGS FELLOWSHIP

I tossed and turned the previous night in anticipation of the following days activities. I was wondering if this fellowship was such a good idea after all. Too late to think about that now. Saturday, April 14, 2018, had finally arrived. It was time to get ready to receive my old and new siblings. I opened my front door so I could see through the storm door as people began to arrive. I busied myself in the kitchen nervously making final preparations. First to arrive were my elder sister Linda and younger sister Joann. While the three of us were in the kitchen preparing food, a tall, dark and handsome gentleman rang the doorbell. I peered excitedly around the corner to see who was there. It was Loren. I immediately knew it was him from the pictures Shawn showed me at our first meeting in March. Loren came in and said hello and then made a gesture with his hand to indicate my height compared to his. He's over six feet tall and I am 5 feet and 4 inches tall. We laughed and hugged and took a selfie with my phone. He went out on the deck to meet my husband and brother-in-law. Next to arrive was Shawn with his two children, his lovely wife, and BF; Adrienne and her husband arrived next; followed by Bobbie with two of her children; and finally, my brother Jade and his wife arrived. Jade is quite the "teddy bear" under his serious facade.

I greeted each one with a warm embrace and introduced myself and old siblings to new siblings. I know, strange, right? I had to introduce myself to my siblings. There was one missing sibling who was out of town on the date of this fellowship. But I'm looking forward to meeting him some time soon. As I played hostess, I tried my best to observe all the family dynamics taking place throughout my home. A song from one of my favorite movies, "The King and I," was playing in my head, "Getting to Know You." Shawn and I explained to the group how we were able to connect on the Ancestry website. It took me right back to that fateful day in February.

My biological father seemed to fit in no matter where he was. I observed him laughing and joking with everyone and having a genuinely good time. He reminds me of a grandfather who has seen and been through a lot in his lifetime and has come to the realization of what's really important. I worked the room and had brief conversations with all of the siblings. There was even a friendly game of Uno Attack going on in the corner of the family room with my new sister Adrienne, my son and niece. My goal as the hostess of this special gathering was to make everyone feel as comfortable as possible. My gosh, there are so many of them! My concern was how would I be able to manage all of this. I didn't know these people, but they seemed to want to get to know me, and that was a marvelous thing. My prayer is that God will help me navigate the waters of building these new relationships with my BF and six new siblings.

After everyone got their fill of good food and good conversation, I asked all the siblings to gather in my living room for a group photo to mark the occasion. Lee took several pictures. Some were of me and the new siblings, some were of me with new and old siblings and the final picture was of all the siblings plus BF. It was our first family photo. Wow! When all was said and done, the day was a success! Everyone ate, drank, laughed and had a wonderful time. It had been a while since BF's kids were all able to get together under one roof and fellowship so I thank God for the opportunity to orchestrate the reunion for them and the union for my two sisters and me. There were a lot of emotions going through my mind but I could feel the presence of God's love covering the occasion. I think this will be the first of more gatherings to come.

I have been referring to my biological father as BF throughout the first ten chapters of this book. Up until this point in my journal, I did not know what I should call him since I had a "dad," who is now deceased. My dad raised me, and provided for me and my two sisters. My dad made a marked impact on my career choice and my life. My dad walked me down the aisle and gave me away on my wedding day. So, I'm trying to figure out what would be appropriate and respectful to call BF. During the fellowship, I heard Shawn refer to BF as "Pops," and that seemed to resonate with me as well. So, I decided that I, too, would call him Pops.

It just astounds me how all my new siblings have rallied around me with all their love and support. I remember Adrienne telling me that I was never going to be able to get rid of her. She is hilarious. She makes me laugh every time we talk. The new siblings have all welcomed me into their hearts as part of their family and I am so grateful. I know this situation could have had a different outcome. My biological father and new siblings could have said they didn't want anything to do with me, but that is not my story. They have welcomed me into their hearts and into their lives. This is an example of my Father in heaven placing me in full view of His love and favor. God is reminding me that as I journey through life, with all its mountains and valleys, sunshine and storms, He will work it all out if I just trust Him. My God is an awesome God! I am blessed, grateful, happy, and amazed. I do have days when I feel some of this is overwhelming and difficult to work through, but I know God is with me every step of the way.

paternal grandmother

Loren and me at the Siblings Fellowship

The day I visited Jade at his home

Meeting Peanut for the first time

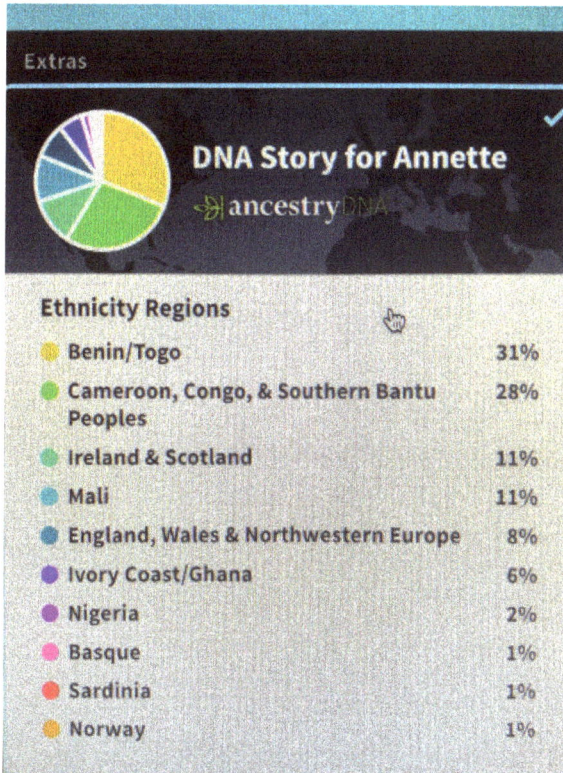

my DNA story

Chapter 12

## LIFE GOES ON IN APRIL & MAY

On Saturday, April 21, 2018, after a morning of being a spectator at my team's tennis match, I was able to share the exciting news about my new family with my tennis sister, Karen. When I gave her the rundown of the number of siblings I now have in my life, she was genuinely excited for me and we had a moment together of high pitched screaming and laughter. It definitely caught me off guard. I have four sisters and four brothers!

On April 22, 2018, I was able to share in my first birthday celebration with my new sister Bobbie. We had dinner in Annapolis, Maryland, with family and friends. It had been a little less than two months since my discovery, and I was involved in family celebrations already. Looks like I jumped into the deep end of the pool right away. Bobbie and I took a selfie at the table, and oh my Lord! The resemblance is quite astonishing.

It was the morning of May 4, 2018, I was praising God for allowing the cast to come off my left arm. I'd be on the court playing tennis again in no time, I hoped. To celebrate the auspicious occasion, I had lunch with Lee and afterwards, bought two pairs of shoes from the DSW, on the sale rack, of course.

May 8th was a special day. It was my biological father's birthday. My new siblings and I met at the Blue Dolphin Restaurant, in Gambrills, Maryland, for a birthday dinner celebration. Being able to celebrate Pop's birthday for the first time was very special and exciting for me. Bobbie brought the delicious birthday cake for dessert and we took lots of pictures to mark the occasion.

On May 10, while taking a shower, I thought about my upcoming breakfast date with Pops, which was planned for the following day, and I started to smile. In that next moment, I thought about my dad and all the great moments he was missing. I somehow felt as though I was betraying my dad by loving another father who I barely knew. I would probably guess that this would be a normal reaction, given the circumstances. And I have allowed myself the freedom and permission to explore these new feelings. The next day, I met Pops for breakfast followed by a trip to the Goodwill Store in search of hidden treasures. We had a great time talking, laughing and just being in the moment together. When it was time for us to part ways, Pops asked if I really had to leave already and said that he had missed a lifetime of hugs. It was an unexpected response. God showed me that Pops loved me because I was his daughter and he was responsible for giving me life. The fact is that he had also missed out on the first 55 years of my life and there was nothing either of us could do about it. I am confident that God will craft this new relationship in a way that is pleasing to Him. And I am hopeful that this new father-daughter relationship will evolve in such a way that God will get all the glory. There's an old saying that goes something like this, "If God brought you to it, He will see you through it."

Chapter 13

## ROAD TRIP!

Now that I was free of that pink cast, I could finally take a trip on my own. I decided to visit my girlfriend, Alicia, who lives in North Carolina. I have always enjoyed driving the five hours to her home. It is usually a peaceful drive, alone with my thoughts and inspirational music. I have my usual stops I make along the way for fuel and supplies which consist of a chocolate donut and a medium sized coffee from the WAWA. My mom called me while I was driving to see how I was doing. I know she and I can't pretend as though nothing has transpired between us, so the communication, at this moment, was somewhat awkward. I am confident that God will set us back on the right path and repair what was broken, at the appointed time. The lesson I am still learning is that forgiveness can be immediate but pain when wounded, (physically or mentally) can take time to heal. Just like my left arm, even though the cast is off, my forearm is still tender and needs time to heal. All in due time and season.

Alicia is so amazingly awesome! I miss not having her closer in proximity since she and her husband moved to North Carolina. When I arrived at her home, and entered the guest room, I was surprised to see a lovely gift bag and card thoughtfully placed on top of the bed. As I opened the envelope and read the card, tears welled up in my eyes as I read the last six words, "I'LL ALWAYS BE HERE FOR YOU." I'm blessed and humbled to have Alicia in my close circle of "iron sharpeners." Proverbs 27:17. Alicia and I spent the following day at the Grandover Resort in Greensboro, North Carolina. We had a delicious buffet breakfast, followed by a good nature walk around the resort's massive property. We had massage treatments at their spa and spent time at the swimming pool. We talked a lot about family, laughed a lot, and had an all around great sistah time. Food, fun, fellowship, and a full spa treatment was just what the doctor ordered.

Chapter 14

## HAPPY FATHER'S DAY!

It is Sunday, June 17, 2018, and it's a special Father's Day. I was open to all the possibilities this day holds for Pops and me. I started out the day by cooking a special breakfast of waffles, eggs, bacon, fruit, orange juice and coffee for the head of my household, Lee. He is my amazing husband, friend and the love of my life. I thank God that he is such a great father. Lee, DJ and I sat down as a family to enjoy each other and watch Lee open his cards and gifts. We then drove to church for their special Father's Day Sunday service. It's always a blessing to see all the dads stand to be recognized. The Women's Praise Team, of which I am a member, sang a song performed by Tasha Cobbs, called "Happy." The song talks about God being the true source of joy, happiness, and wholeness. It is difficult to sing this song and not experience the joy and peace of the Lord.

Later that afternoon, Lee, DJ and I traveled to my brother Loren's house for a Father's Day dinner and celebration. We arrived before most people. Pops arrived with my brother Shawn and Shawn's son Michael. Pops greeted me with a huge hug as I wished him a Happy Father's Day for the very first time. It felt as though time stood still just long enough to take it all in and breathe again. Everyone present enjoyed a wonderful fellowship, lots of scrumptious food, and lots of laughter. I was still getting used to being around my new family as I'm sure they were getting used to being around me. Only God could have made this unimaginable union a reality in all our lives. In my mind, I could hear Shirley Caesar singing "This joy I have, the world didn't give it to me." I have been enjoying the ride.

Galatians 5:22 *"But the fruit of the Spirit is love, JOY..."*(NIV)

The following Friday, my son, DJ and I drove to Pops' house for a visit. It was time for a road trip to the cemetery to visit the gravesite of my paternal grandmother and two brothers. It was a cloudy, overcast day but it had not yet begun to rain. Pops had prepared for the weather by bringing along a large golf umbrella. He had also purchased a sufficient number of beautiful flowers consisting of daisies and roses which were to be placed at the different family gravesites. Once we arrived at the cemetery, we donned our rain jackets and walked over to the designated section. Pops gave DJ and me a little history lesson about the family members who were buried there. It began to drizzle, but we were on a mission to pay our respects and did not let the impending rain interfere with our plans. We placed flowers at the graveside of grandmother Madeline, and brothers Keenan and Michael. DJ and I spent a few quiet moments in reflection. In some way, it was closure to the loss of my grandmother, Madeline, who everyone said I favored, and my brothers, Keenan and Michael, who I did not know at the time of their passing but for whom I would still mourn their loss. Although I didn't know them, it was a way to pay homage until we meet again. Pops placed flowers at the graveside of his wife and spent a few quiet moments in reflection.

The following day I sent Pops a text letting him know how much I had enjoyed spending time with him. He sent me the following response: "Getting to know you, getting to know all about you." (From the musical: "The King and I"). All I could do was laugh out loud! I tried to trip him up by sending him the next line of the song, "Getting to like you, getting to hope you like me." But, he followed up with the third line of the song. I gave up at that point. My Pops is a hoot! I found out that he grew up listening to all kinds of music, so I'm sure he can "one up me" on most tunes.

Chapter 15

## WHO IS MY FAMILY

I spent the summer visiting with Pops and spending time with my new siblings and meeting new nieces and nephews. I also spent the summer showing up at my aunt's 80th surprise birthday party and my cousin's surprise beach party. These two relatives are related to the dad who raised me and they didn't know about our non-DNA relationship. At my aunt's party, I remember trying really hard not to feel disconnected. Then it happened. One of my cousins made a comment of how I didn't look like my dad's side of the family and that comment made the night very awkward for me. A couple of weeks later I attended my cousin's birthday celebration at Sandy Point State Park and Beach in Annapolis, Maryland. As I sat under the pavillion with my aunt and cousins, laughing, talking and eating barbeque, the Lord whispered in my ear the answer to my query concerning my dad's side of the family. God said to me, although they were not related to me by any DNA, they were related to me by something much more valuable and important. We were related by the love we had for each other, through Christ, and that meant much more than any DNA result. This kind of love is priceless.

> John 13:34-35 A new command I give you: Love one another. As I have loved you, so you must love one another. By this everyone will know that you are my disciples, if you love one another. (NIV)

Chapter 16

## AUTUMN & WINTER MILESTONES

Autumn had arrived as evidenced by the spectacular array of colors on the leaves and the coolness of the morning air announcing the end of summer. Football season was in full swing and I love me some football! It's a passion I developed as a child while watching my dad and his friends gather around the television and yell at all the plays every Sunday afternoon. I decided to drive to Pop's house one Sunday afternoon with two crab cake sandwiches in hand, to watch the Washington Redskins vs. the Green Bay Packers game. We sat in the dining room, eating lunch and watching the game. I laughed as his chair rolled about with every movement of the pigskin toward the opponents goal line. He said if the dining room table was not there, he would probably roll out the door while watching the plays. I laughed even harder. I will always remember that day with fondness. Thank you Lord for allowing me to spend quality time with my biological father.

In the blink of an eye, it was Thanksgiving Day! My husband, son and I spent the morning at church, packing up and delivering food to those in need, followed by dinner at Pops' house with my new siblings and family. It was good to see what traditions they had built and adopted over their lifetime. Pops blessed the food and asked me to say a prayer, after him, to commemorate this special occasion, our first Thanksgiving together. As I began to pray, I became overwhelmed with gratefulness as God showed me again how much He loves me and my family. He's a good, good, Father, that's who He is!

*Psalm 100:4-5 Enter His gates with thanksgiving*
*and His courts with praise; give thanks to Him*
*and praise his name. For the Lord is good and his*
*love endures forever; his faithfulness continues*
*through all generations.(NIV)*

*Psalm 147:3 He heals the brokenhearted and*
*binds up their wounds. (NIV)*

In four short weeks, the Christmas holiday season was upon us. DJ and I spent Christmas Eve visiting Pops and showering him with our first Christmas gifts. We spent Christmas day delivering gifts to cousins, nieces and nephews. I watched my son play the older cousin role as he helped one of his new younger cousins put together one of his toys. It was a sight to behold. We drove to my new sister, Adrienne's house for a surprise visit. We then returned home to enjoy Christmas dinner with our neighbors. It was a blessed day in the Lord. My son commented that he truly enjoyed visiting his new family. As I look back over this year, I can see the hand of God was all over me and supplying all my needs. I have survived the valley and am still surviving because of God.

Chapter 17

## HAPPY NEW YEAR!

My brother Shawn telephoned me this morning, the first day of 2019, to wish me a Happy New Year and to remind me that this was my very first New Year with my new family. That thought sent an overwhelming wave of excitement over me. I felt extremely blessed to know all of my new siblings: Adrienne, Loren, Jade, Bobbie, Shawn, and Peanut, and my biological father on this New Year. What initially didn't look like a blessing to me on that fateful day in February of 2018, turned out to be more than I could have ever hoped for. I am so grateful to know my biological father, affectionately known as Pops, and my new siblings.

The following day I had a great conversation with mom. Although I can't imagine what she must be going through,  as a mom, I agree that no parent wants to intentionally hurt their child. I love my mom with all my heart and I pray that God's unconditional love will always shine new light on our relationship. I explained to mom that finding out the truth about who I am has forever changed me for the better. I am getting to know my father and siblings. They have been warm, kind and loving towards me. It has been an absolute joy and a tremendous blessing. I think it's a miracle from God that I'm not angry, although a little sad at times. When sadness approaches, I usually find opportunities to turn that feeling into God's joy and hope for our future. And I know that His plan is always so much better than mine.

> Jeremiah 29:11 "For I know the plans I have for you,"
> declares the Lord, "plans to prosper you and not to
> harm you, plans to give you hope and a future." (NIV)

On the way home from my son's piano lessons, I called Pops. I could feel him smiling through the phone. We talked and laughed as usual.

48

Today is my anniversary!  It is February 27, 2019. One year ago, today, I discovered the other half of my biological family tree on Ancestry DNA. After a year of uncertainty and identity crisis, I've been on the mend, piece by piece surrounded by truth, love, joy, family and friends. A lot of the original pieces of information about my identity have changed, and it's okay. I have replaced those pieces with new pieces that are full of exciting new knowledge and exciting new information about myself, my DNA and my family. It's been a blessing to be able to dive into this new information about my roots as I continue to discover who I am on the ancestry tree. What began as fragmented pieces of my life has turned into a peaceful journey and I am forever thankful to God as it is still unfolding. I now have an overabundance of family from my mom's side, my dad's side, and my biological father's side and I love them all. I was lost but now I'm found, was blind but now I see. Thank you Lord for your amazing grace!

Chapter 18

## FULL CIRCLE

My son's annual piano recital was Saturday, March 30 and I invited the usual recital family members. However, this year, I had the privilege of inviting Pops as well as my new siblings to come out and support their newest member of the family. I am never certain who will be in attendance due to the early recital start time of 8:30 on a Saturday morning. My sister Joann with daughter Maya and my new sister Bobbie came in and sat beside each other. That was a beautiful sight to behold. Next to enter was my eldest sister Linda with Jordan, my nephew. Then came, my uncle Melvin with my niece Skyy and nephews Josiah and EJ in tow. My mom and two of her sisters entered next and found their seats. DJ's performance was exceptional as he performed, "Sing Your Praise to the Lord," words and music by Richard Mullins. He then played an original piece based on the story of Lazarus, found in the book of John, chapter 11 in the Holy Bible. At the conclusion of the recital, I turned around to see DJ walking toward his grandfather, Pops, his uncles Loren, Jade, and Shawn with his wife Dominese and DJ's brother, Joseph. Then my old family walked over to meet my new family and the introductions began. It was a bit overwhelming and somewhat awkward but I was thankful they were all able to come and support DJ during his recital. DJ was very excited to see them and I was excited for him. Then it happened. My mom came over and she and Pops had a brief conversation where he told her she did a great job raising her three girls. Linda teased them about the comment and then had them to continue to stand together for a picture. Linda said it was just good timing. I said, "God timing is always perfect timing."

I reflected on DJ's recital the previous year in 2018, when I was just beginning to process the news of a biological father and it was all I could do to maintain some semblance of normalcy, holding it together for my son's recital and getting through the day in one piece! What a difference a year makes. I know my journey is not over, but I have more peace and more ridiculously crazy, silly, loving family members to enjoy and build lasting relationships with than I ever could have imagined.

> May the God of peace be with you all. Amen Romans 15:33
> (AMP)


On Saturday, April 6, 2019, I finally got a chance to meet the youngest new sibling nicknamed, Peanut. We agreed to meet at a donut shop in Virginia. I arrived a few minutes early and went inside to wait for his arrival. While in the ladies room washing my hands, Peanut telephoned to advise that he was about to enter the donut shop. As I exited the ladies room, I saw a gentleman standing just inside the front door of the shop with his back to me. As he turned around, we both smiled and hugged and laughed. We had the very same large eyes and long eyelashes. I suppose those eyes must be a dominant gene in our DNA. We chose a comfortable area to sit and talk and enjoy our donut selections. I shared the story of my biological father discovery and Peanut shared his discovery story as well. Peanut was just a teenager when he met our father so I'm sure he had a much different experience. As with the other new siblings, I'm looking forward to developing my relationship as Peanut's oldest sister.

# Chapter 19

## TAKEAWAYS

You are guaranteed to experience several different emotions after your discovery of a NPE "Non-Parental Event," also referred to as, "Not Parent Expected." Here are some takeaways I would like to share with you that helped me:

- You are not alone.

- Remember that your journey is your journey. Let no one tell you how you should be feeling in these extraordinary circumstances. If they have not personally experienced this kind of trauma, they have no way of fully comprehending it.

- You may experience fear and anxiety and you may feel emotionally drained at times. Intimacy with God will be your source of strength.

- You are neither a secret nor a mistake. You are a human being created in God's image.

- I encourage you to seek professional counseling if necessary. Or find a support group.

- How do I tell others? Whether you get to develop relationships with your new family members, or not, remember this is your journey. It really isn't anyone else's business. You can share your discovery with whom you choose. For others, it is just information, but, for you, it has been life changing. And you're dealing with it as best you can, day by day.

- Keep pressing forward in Jesus' name. He is your strength and sustainer, your fortress and rock, your hiding place and help, your joy, faithful Father and friend. God will be whatever you need Him to be if you continue to draw near to Him in all circumstances.

- Don't be stagnant. Move from hurt to hope! There is life after this type of trauma. God's word is filled with hope. So be hopeful and stay hopeful.

- We all need special people in our lives to help us live out this life. I pray that God will bless you with the special people you stand in need of to help encourage you along the way.

- Continue building a strong foundation in Jesus, our Lord and Savior.

- It is important to know your parents' DNA, not only for health reasons but for dating/marriage as well. Thought: What if I had dated or married one of my brothers? Then what?

- Forgiveness is the key to moving forward. Let go of the anger. Anger only hurts YOU. Refuse to spend your valuable time on anger.

- If you turn your situation over to your heavenly Father, you will see God's power and presence in your life on a completely different level. You will get to know God in ways you have never known Him before.

- God will move through your situation in a loving, caring, mighty way like only a Sovereign God could.

- Refuse to be a victim. Remember, you are more than a conqueror through Christ Jesus our Lord and Savior. You can live victoriously!

- Only things that are hidden have power over you. (Joyce Meyer)

- Your identity ultimately lies in Christ alone.

> Acts 17:28 For in Him we live and move and have our being.
> As some of your own poets have said, 'We are his offspring
> (children) (NIV)

- In the end, if you believe in Jesus Christ as your Lord and Savior, you win!

## ACKNOWLEDGEMENTS:

To my Lord and Savior Jesus Christ for being my everything, always.

My Husband, Lee for loving me through all the craziness, heartache, excitement, and loving me everyday of my life. I love you more today than yesterday.

My handsome teenager, DJ for all your wonderful hugs this past year and beyond.

My oldest son, Joseph and my daughter, Raylynn for your loving spirit. Looking forward to seeing what God has instore for you.

My brother, Shawn for being on Ancestry.com all those years and choosing to be such a caring protector since February 27, 2018.

Alicia for being my confidant and life long friend, and iron sharpener. Thank you for crying with me and walking through this journey with me.

Karen for your excitement and honesty on the pages.

Shurett for your wisdom in seeing so many possibilities and blessings.

Millicent for all your prayers and discernment.

Richard Cohen for being a mentor and brother-in-Christ.

Linda and Joann for your sibling love and support.

Adrienne, Loren, Jade, Bobbie and Peanut for your spontaneous love, hugs and support.

Dad & Mom for raising your three girls to be the women we are today.

Pops for your love and extraordinary laughter.

## About the Author:

Her name is Annette James. She's a daughter, a sister, a wife, a mother, and retired law enforcement officer. She grew up in Washington, D.C., in the southeast neighborhood in Anacostia known as Barry Farms. She currently resides in Maryland with her husband of 20 years and their teenage son. As a member of the Women's Praise Team at New Vision Church, Annette loves to worship the Lord with all her heart and encourages others to do so as well. Her favorite pastimes are spending time with her family, acting, tutoring children in reading, writing poetry and inspirational songs, watching a good movie, and traveling.

## GOD'S MASTERPIECE

*Created in His image*
*A one and only gem*
*Fashioned in the secret place*
*Molded to be like Him*
*There has never been*
*Nor will there ever be*
*A person on this earth*
*With the DNA of me*
*Crafted by design*
*Created for a purpose*
*He has shown me some of my gifts*
*But I'm just scratching the surface*
*What are you waiting for?*
*Draw close to Him and see*
*The awesome purpose of your life*
*God created you to be*

*AJ*

www.ingramcontent.com/pod-product-compliance
Lightning Source LLC
Chambersburg PA
CBHW041301040426
42334CB00028BA/3122